HOW THEY LIVED

A PLANTATION SLAVE

ROBIN MAY

Illustrated by
Mark Bergin

Wayland

HOW THEY LIVED

An American Pioneer Family
A Colonial American Merchant
A Crusading Knight
An Edwardian Household
A Family in World War II
An Ice Age Hunter
A Medieval Serf
A Plantation Slave
A Roman Centurion
A Saxon Farmer
A Slave in Ancient Greece
A Victorian Factory Worker
A Viking Sailor

First published in 1986 by
Wayland (Publishers) Limited
61 Western Road, Hove
East Sussex BN3 1JD, England

British Library Cataloguing in Publication Data
May, Robin
A Plantation slave. — (How they lived)
1. Slaves — Southern States — History/Juvenile Literature
2. Southern States — Social life and customs — Colonial period, ca. 1600-1755 — Juvenile literature 3. Southern States — Social life and customs — 1755-1965 — Juvenile literature.
1. Title II. Bergin, Mark III. Series 305.5 '67' 0975 E444B.

ISBN 0 85078 578 2

Typeset by Planagraphic Typesetters Limited
Printed in Italy by G. Canale & C.S.p.A., Turin
Bound in the UK by The Bath Press, Avon

CONTENTS

PEOPLE FOR SALE 4

THE SLAVE TRADE 6

CROSSING THE OCEAN 8

A SLAVE AUCTION 10

SLAVE OWNERS 12

FAMILY LIFE 14

WORKING IN THE FIELDS 16

OTHER WORK 18

REST, FOOD AND DRINK 20

RELIGION 22

PUNISHMENT 24

ESCAPE! 26

SLAVE REVOLTS 28

THE END OF SLAVERY 30

GLOSSARY 31

MORE BOOKS TO READ 31

INDEX 32

PEOPLE FOR SALE

He was 10 years old and he stood beside his weeping mother. They were blacks and both were for sale. Moments before, the boy had seen his father sold to a white man, who had looked him over as if he were an animal. Then his father was dragged away, looking back in agony at his little family. Now it was time for the mother and her child to be sold — separately . . .

The splitting up of families was

perhaps the worst thing that could happen to slaves in the southern states of the USA 150 years or so ago. At least death was a release from misery.

Slavery itself is as old as mankind, and it still flourishes today in many parts of the world. But it grew very rapidly in the 1600s. Blacks from Africa were taken in large numbers to South America, the West Indies and England's North American colonies. When these colonies declared themselves independent in 1776 there were slaves in all of them. But most were in the southern states. By 1860, there were three million slaves in the South. They were needed to work on tobacco, sugar, rice and, especially, cotton plantations.

Above *A cargo of black slaves arriving in Jamestown in 1619. This was about the time when the trade in slaves between Africa and the Americas began to flourish.*

THE SLAVE TRADE

Just twenty-five years after Christopher Columbus reached the New World in 1492 the first unhappy African slaves were taken there by Spaniards. Soon other nations joined in this trade in human beings, including the Portuguese, the French, the Dutch and the English.

The slave trade started to boom in the 1600s when a number of seafaring nations acquired colonies in the West Indies, which were rich in sugar.

The trade was well organized, especially by the British in the eighteenth century. But it was only possible because African rulers were willing to sell their people to Europeans.

A ship would sail from a British or European port to the west coast of Africa. It would be laden with goods for local chiefs. They then handed

Slaves being marched from their homes to the nearest port.

over first people captured from other tribes, and later members of their own tribe, in payment.

The slaves were taken across the Atlantic in nightmarish conditions, then sold. The ships returned to Europe laden with sugar, cotton, tobacco and other goods. This trade was called the Triangular Trade, as a look at the map will explain.

Above *Slaves wait on a quayside before being taken to auction.*

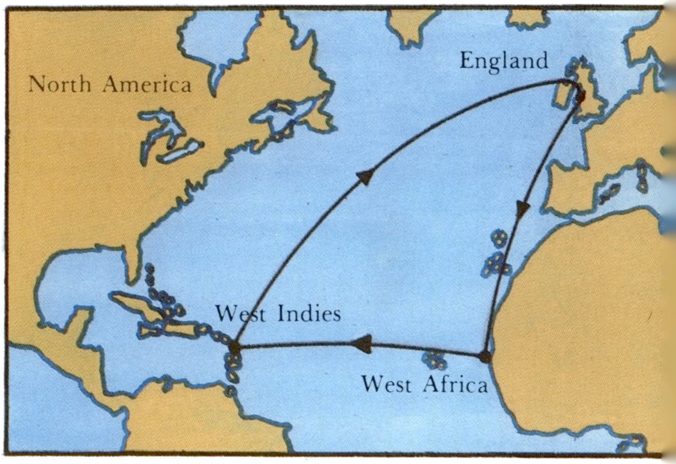

The 'Triangular Trade' between Europe, Africa and the Americas.

CROSSING THE OCEAN

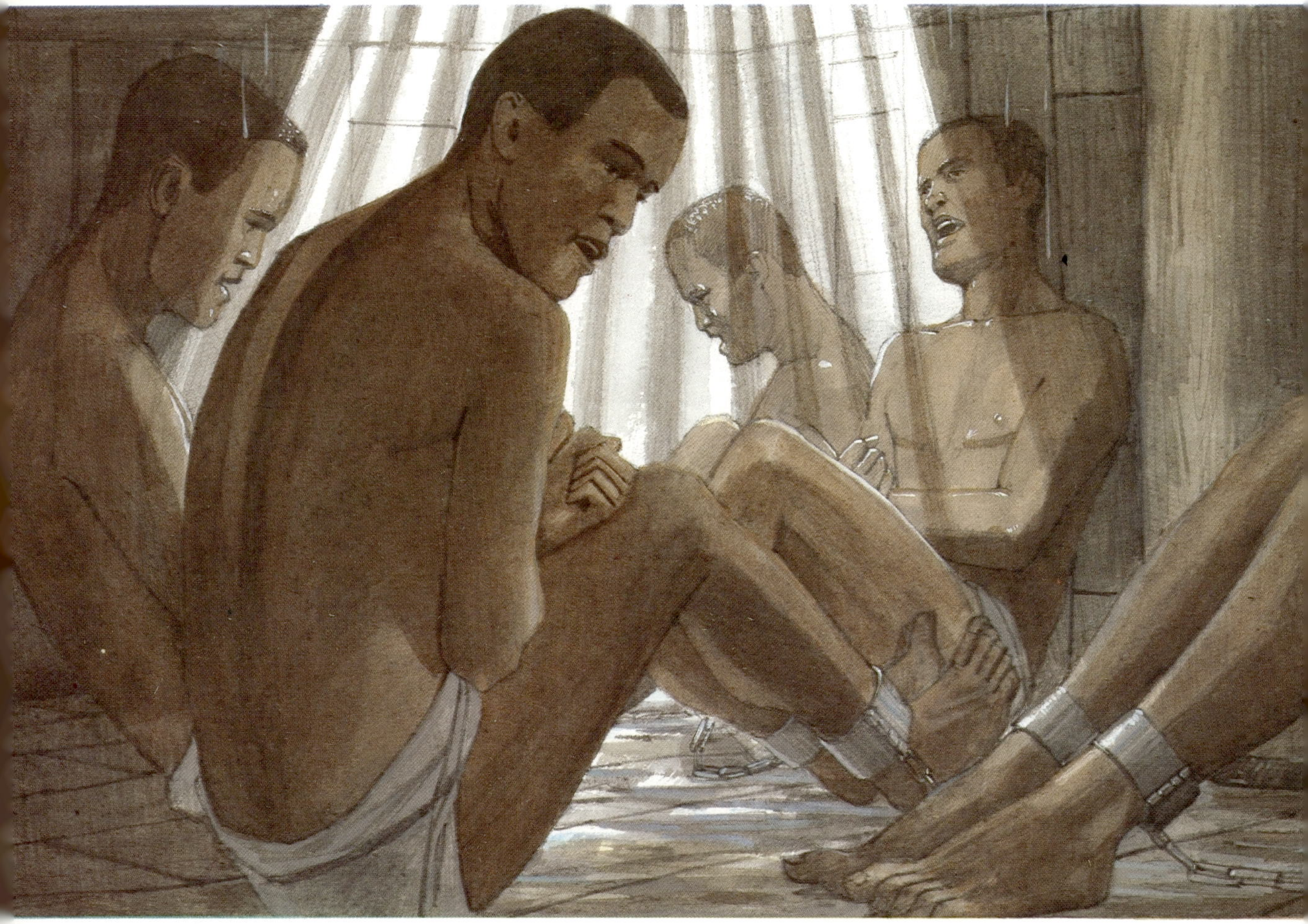

Slaves were shipped across the Atlantic in terrible conditions.

Slave ships were floating hells. The largest of them could carry 700 slaves. These were packed below decks. Each male slave was chained to his neighbour in dungeons 1.5 metres (5 feet) or less high. A slave's living space was the size of a coffin. Women and children were crammed in elsewhere, but at least they were not chained.

All slaves were taken up on deck twice daily to be fed. They were also exercised, being forced to jump up and down, helped along by whips. During exercises the ship's crew cleaned out the slaves' horrible prison decks. Then the slaves were driven back below.

Some captains overpacked their vessels with slaves to ensure that there would be plenty left alive despite deaths from overcrowding. Others carried fewer, hoping to have more to sell because of the slightly better conditions. The average voyage took five awful weeks, but some took much longer. Slavery itself was rarely as horrible as the slaves' journey to it.

Below *A poster advertising the sale of slaves.*

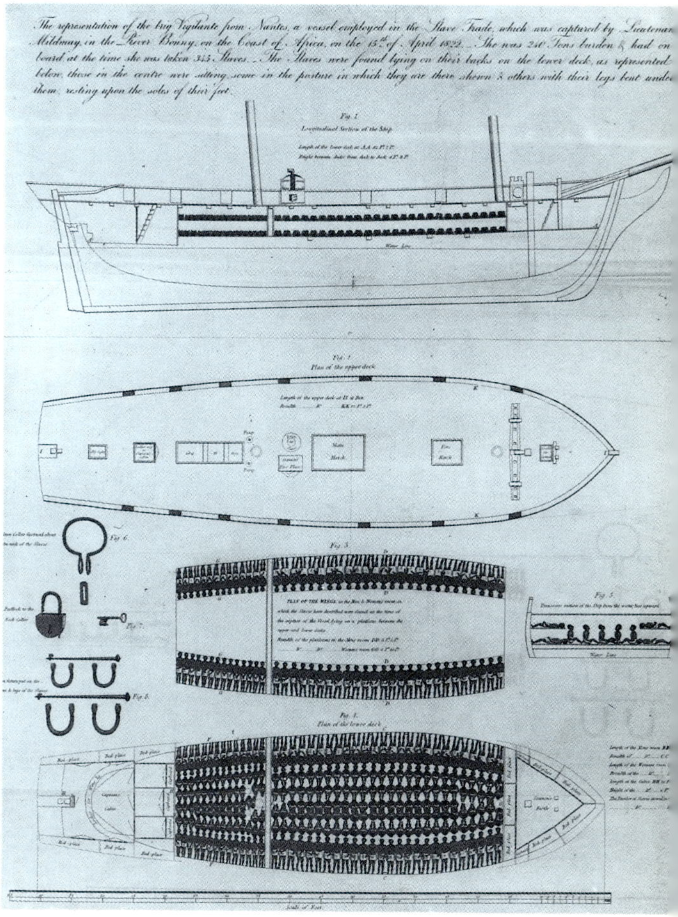

Above *A diagram of a slave ship showing how the slaves were packed in for their nightmare journey across the Atlantic.*

In the last days of the voyage slaves were given better food. Their sores, received from chains, boils and beatings, were hidden by a mixture of gunpowder and rust — to make the slaves more marketable.

A Slave Auction

A slave, like an animal, a piece of furniture, or a bale of cotton, could be bought or sold whenever his or her master wished it.

Before an auction, the slaves were naturally made to look their best. They were cleaner than most could ever hope to be in their slave dwellings, and they were given fresh clothes. Old slaves were sometimes made to look younger, grey hairs being plucked out or blacked. Buyers would examine them as if they were animals. Their backs were checked to see if they had been flogged for being 'troublemakers'.

There were always plenty of buyers at slave auctions, for they were widely advertised by posters and by notices in local papers.

One slave, Josiah Henson, later described his own sale when he was a boy. His master died and the plantation had to be sold. First his brother and sister were sold off, then his mother. She flung herself at the buyer's feet, imploring him to buy Josiah, her youngest child, too. The buyer kicked her away.

Opposite *Families always dreaded being split up after an auction.*

Below *A slave auction in progress.*

SLAVES

SLAVE OWNERS

Slavery is brutal, but not all slave owners were. With a kindly owner, slaves could hope to enjoy better living conditions than many poor whites endured. Some slaves, usually house slaves, were given their freedom if they had served their master well.

Other owners were different. They were harsh and cruel themselves and they let their overseers persecute, and sometimes kill, their slaves. A slave had no rights at all. His master had the power of life and death over him.

One slave named Joe recalled how he was regularly hired out by his master to oversee one of his friend's slaves. He worked so well that the man bought him from his master for a huge sum. His new master said he was going to flog him. The slave asked why after all the good service he had done. 'The first thing my niggers have to learn is that I am master,' the man said. He then warned the slave that he'd be flogged to death if he resisted.

Joe took his 'punishment' but made up his mind to escape to the northern states where slavery had by then been banned, and did so. He was one of the lucky ones.

FAMILY LIFE

Family life meant much to slaves, but a slave marriage often ended in misery. For, though slaves were allowed to marry, the marriage was not recognized by white law. As we have seen, slave families were often split up.

The object of a slave marriage — as far as the whites were concerned — was for slaves to produce more slaves. They could then be used by their owner or sold off. For some slaves, however, especially those lucky enough to work for good masters, marriage saved them from despair.

White masters and overseers all too often took advantage of black slave girls. Their children would then be sold as slaves.

A slave family outside their home.

Above *Booker Washington, a slave who later became a teacher.*

An ex-slave called Booker Washington recalled how he and his family never sat down at the table together to eat. The children were given their meals 'very much as dumb animals get theirs. It was a piece of bread here and a scrap of meat there.' He lived to become a teacher and a spokesman for his people.

Many slaves died young. Their one-room shacks, often shared by several families, were germ-ridden, and let in

the cold and the rain. Killer diseases spread like wildfire. It is thought that only four out of every 100 slaves lived to the age of 60.

Above and below *Slave homes were one-room shacks which often housed more than one slave family. They were poorly built and cold.*

WORKING IN THE FIELDS

Slaves became field hands by the age of 12; many started when they were just 10. In the seventeenth and eighteenth centuries most of those in the South worked on tobacco, rice, sugar and indigo plantations. Then, in 1793, an inventor named Eli Whitney made a machine called a 'cotton gin'. Cotton had always been slowly separated from its seed by hand. The gin separated the tough seeds from the white fibre swiftly. The textile industry in America and Britain needed this fibre and the cotton business boomed. So did slavery, as cotton became the South's chief crop.

Male and female field hands worked from sunrise to sunset. Some were allowed a short rest at noon. Some masters even made their slaves work at night when the moon was full. Slaves wore rough, uncomfortable clothes and were issued with coarsely made shoes once a year.

Slaves at work in the cotton fields.

A steam-driven cotton gin in action. Slaves gather the cotton into bales.

An overseer kept watch over the slaves to make sure that none was slacking. Sometimes he had the help of black assistant overseers, complete with whips. The field hands were encouraged to sing as this improved their will to work. When there was no cotton to plant or pick, or fields to plough, they worked at other jobs on the land.

OTHER WORK

Above *These slaves are loading bales of cotton on to riverboats, the main form of bulk transport on the Mississippi River.*

Some slaves were skilled craftsmen, working as carpenters or blacksmiths. Slaves were also made to work in factories, on railroads, riverboats and — worse than any other job — in coal mines. The luckiest slaves of all — unless their masters and mistresses were very cruel — were the house slaves.

Even for these slaves there was always the threat of flogging or being sold, but their life was good by slave standards. They enjoyed better living conditions than field hands. A slave husband might be the smartly dressed butler, his wife the cook or the mistress's personal maid.

House slaves could hear what was going on in the world by keeping their ears open. The personal slaves would not have to cringe to their master and mistress, or lower their gaze and their voices, as all other slaves had to in the presence of whites.

Another advantage of being a house slave was that he or she was more likely to be freed than the other slaves. For the field hands, escape was the only real chance of liberty.

House slaves enjoyed a better life than those working in the fields.

REST, FOOD AND DRINK

Rest is not the ideal word to describe a slave's time off, because it was often the rest of total exhaustion. For most slaves, Sunday was their day of rest. Some slaves got Saturday afternoon off as well. Their owners encouraged them to do a little washing or fishing or gardening in their spare time.

Slaves were never well fed, though

Slaves spent what little spare time they had gardening or fishing.

house slaves usually ate better than field hands. Slaves fared worse on a rundown plantation. The ex-slave Charles Ball wrote that in such a place 'nothing is allowed to the poor negro, but his peck of corn per week, without the sauce of a salt herring, or even a little salt itself.' Short rations were often used by slave owners as a form of punishment.

The field hand was likely to get a ration of corn and fat pork. If he could catch a fish or an animal he would fare better, and most slaves raised vegetables in the patches of ground they were given. Their poor diet laid them wide open to diseases and their teeth were usually rotten.

To cheer themselves up, slaves danced when they could, and went to prayer meetings, but what they wanted most in their time off was to do nothing.

Sometimes, slaves held dances to cheer themselves up.

RELIGION

Many slaves found comfort in religion. They could look forward to a world to come after death where they would be free. Some of the slaves who came from Africa brought their old religions to America with them. These sometimes became mixed together with Christianity, and both would help the slaves get through their harsh and wretched existence.

Frederick Douglass, a slave who escaped to become a great figure in his people's fight for their rights, prayed: 'I am left in the hottest hell of unending slavery. Oh God, save me — why am I a slave?'

Slaves, and their white owners, listen to a sermon being preached.

Slaves often had to bury their dead at night.

Isabel Baumfree, an escaped slave, told northerners how God meant her to travel up and down the land, and travel she did telling people the facts of slavery.

Slaves often had to bury the dead at night so as not to interfere with their work. Later, they would hold a memorial service and rejoice that the dead person was free. To many slaves, religion meant singing. Their songs were called 'spirituals'. Some negro spirituals, like *Deep River* and *Swing Low Sweet Chariot,* are still sung today.

PUNISHMENT

Flogging was the standard form of punishment for slaves.

Though the worst form of punishment for a slave family was to be split up and sold, the standard punishment was a flogging. Male slaves, and sometimes women, too, were savagely beaten. As well as masters and overseers, professional 'slave breakers' flogged the slaves for a fee.

A rawhide lash was used for most floggings, the number of lashes being between fifteen and twenty. Recaptured slaves and other 'criminals' could receive more than 100 lashes and have their backs beaten to a pulp.

A master who did not wish to lose his slave from infection had salt water thrown over the wounds. The agony of this was even worse than the flogging had been. Other punishments included being shackled with chains, and being forced into an iron collar from which prongs stuck out. These stopped the unfortunate victim lying down to rest.

One of the worst crimes was for a slave to strike a white man. The slave might easily be flogged to death as an example to the others. The slave Josiah Henson's father tried to defend his mother from the attentions of an overseer. He received 100 lashes, then had his right ear nailed to the whipping post and struck from his body.

Sometimes, slaves were put in the stocks as a punishment.

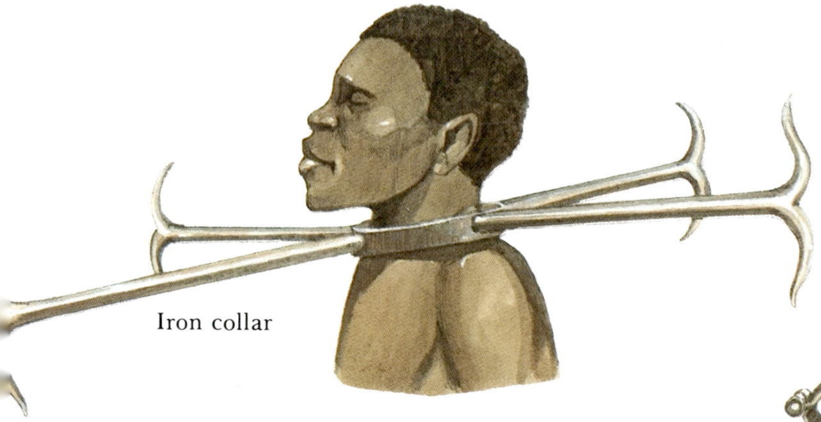

Iron collar

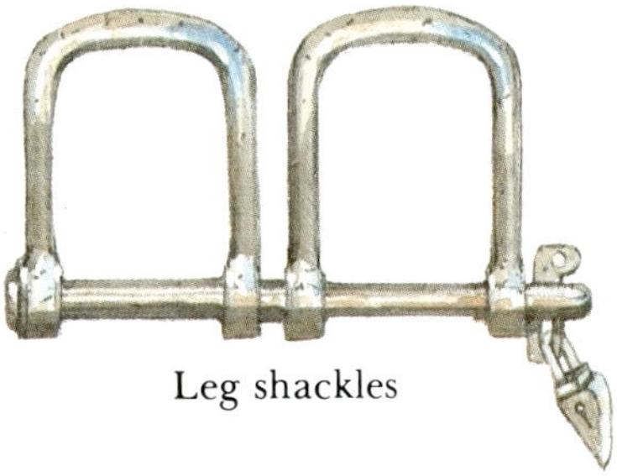

Leg shackles

Hand cuffs

Some of the awful devices used to keep slaves in order.

ESCAPE!

Naturally, very many slaves, especially those living near the free states, tried to escape. They risked savage punishment if caught, but hundreds succeeded each year.

Many were helped by a daring escape organization called the Underground Railroad. This was run by white 'abolitionists' and blacks, who helped escapers and ran safe hiding places for the runaways. One of the most daring helpers was an ex-slave called Harriet Tubman, who led more than 300 to freedom.

Right *Harriet Tubman.*
Below The Liberator *was the journal of the abolitionists.*

Ex-slaves were not always welcomed in the North, especially by white workers fearing for their jobs. The North was not always a safe haven either. To try and prevent a split between North and South, a cruel law was passed that allowed those who had escaped to freedom to be sent back South. Slaves had to reach Canada to be really safe. Slavery had been abolished in the British Empire (of which Canada was a part) in 1833.

Escaped slaves publicly told the facts about slavery to northerners and to Europeans. 'I stole this head, these limbs, this body from my master, and ran off with them,' Frederick Douglass told an anti-slavery meeting.

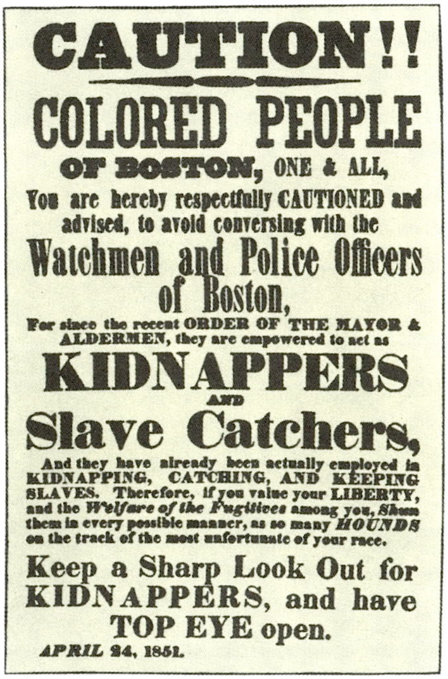
CAUTION!!

COLORED PEOPLE

OF BOSTON, ONE & ALL,

You are hereby respectfully CAUTIONED and advised, to avoid conversing with the

Watchmen and Police Officers of Boston,

For since the recent ORDER OF THE MAYOR & ALDERMEN, they are empowered to act as

KIDNAPPERS

AND

Slave Catchers,

And they have already been actually employed in KIDNAPPING, CATCHING, AND KEEPING SLAVES. Therefore, if you value your LIBERTY, and the *Welfare of the Fugitives* among you, *Shun* them in every possible manner, as so many *HOUNDS* on the track of the most unfortunate of your race.

Keep a Sharp Look Out for KIDNAPPERS, and have TOP EYE open.

APRIL 24, 1851.

Right *A poster warning runaway slaves in Boston to beware of being recaptured.*

Below *Runaway slaves faced awful punishments if captured.*

SLAVE REVOLTS

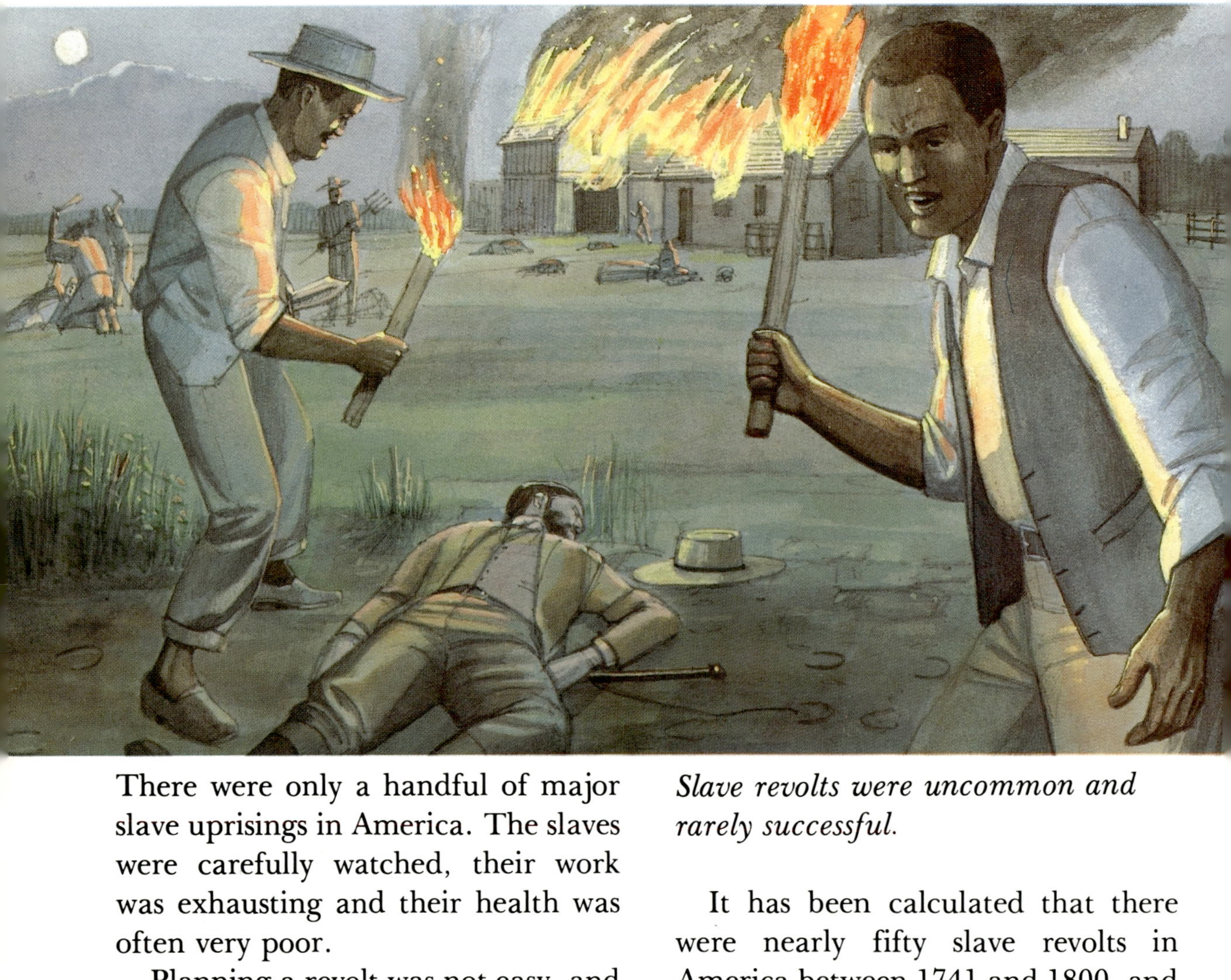

Slave revolts were uncommon and rarely successful.

There were only a handful of major slave uprisings in America. The slaves were carefully watched, their work was exhausting and their health was often very poor.

Planning a revolt was not easy, and because of the campaign of the abolitionists in the North, slave owners were on the alert.

It has been calculated that there were nearly fifty slave revolts in America between 1741 and 1800, and 210 between 1791 and 1856, but most of these were small.

Even the biggest was not a large-scale revolt, though it created terror among whites. It was led by Nat Turner, who believed that God was on his side. Using axes and hatchets, then guns that they seized, Nat and perhaps seventy other slaves killed some fifty white men, women and children. Then they escaped to the woods and stayed free for six weeks.

The rebellion ended when Nat Turner and sixteen others were caught and hanged. During the rebellion many innocent blacks were brutally treated by whites, and afterwards things became even worse for slaves. Laws were passed restricting freedom of the press and of speech.

The discovery and recapture of Nat Turner.

THE END OF SLAVERY

By the middle of the nineteenth century, the campaign against slavery had reached a peak. But the opposition from northern abolitionists only made people in the South more obstinate. The American nation began to tear itself apart. The climax came with the Civil war (1861-65). Although the war was not fought only over the issue of slavery, without it, there would have been no war.

In 1863, President Abraham Lincoln, the leader of the northern states, proclaimed all slaves free. But the war dragged on for another two years. Eventually the North won and the slaves were freed. However, Lincoln was later murdered and the freed slaves were often little better off than before. Not until quite recently have the black descendants of the slaves become truly equal with white Americans.

Freed slaves making their way north following Lincoln's proclamation.

GLOSSARY

Abolitionist Someone who wants to abolish or do away with something. There were a number anti-slavery groups in the North. The most angry and active group was called the abolitionists.

Auction A public sale where people bid for the items being sold. The goods go to the highest bidder.

Civil War A war between two groups of people within one country. The American Civil War (1861-65) was fought by the United States against eleven southern states that had broken away from the Union. There were many differences between North and South, but it was slavery that caused the drift to war.

Colony A country owned, governed and settled by people from another country.

Indigo A plant producing a deep blue dye.

Memorial service A church service held in memory of someone after they have died and have been buried.

Negro A black person. The word means black man in Spanish. Nowadays the term 'black' is preferred.

New World The continents of North and South America, which which were 'new' to the explorers of the fifteenth and sixteenth centuries.

Nigger A slang word for a black or negro. It is usually used as a term of abuse.

Overseer A supervisor or manager.

Plantation A large farm or estate.

Rawhide Coarse leather.

MORE BOOKS TO READ

Non-fiction

John F. Bayliss, *Black Slave Narratives* (Collier-Macmillan, 1970).

Philip Clark, *Abraham Lincoln* (Wayland, 1983).

William C. Davis, *Brother Against Brother — The War Begins* (Time-Life Books, 1983).

J. C. Furnas, *The Americans* (Longman, 1969).

Anne Mountfield, *The Slave Trade* (Wayland, 1973).

Fiction

Stowe, Harriet Beecher, *Uncle Tom's Cabin* (Bantam Books, 1983).

INDEX

Abolitionists 26, 28, 30
Africa 5, 6, 22

Ball, Charles 21
Baumfree, Isabel 23

Children 4, 8, 14
Civil War 30
Clothes 10, 16
Columbus, Christopher 6
Cotton 5, 7, 16-17
Cotton gin 16

Douglass, Frederick 22, 27

Escape 19, 26-27

Family life 14-15
Field hands 16-17, 19, 21
Food 9, 14, 20-21
Freedom 13, 19, 29, 30

Health 8, 9, 14-15, 21, 28
Henson, Josiah 10, 25
House slaves 18-19, 21

Lincoln, Abraham, President 30
Living conditions 8, 9, 14-15, 19

Marriage 14

Overseers 13, 14, 16, 17, 24, 25

Plantations 5, 10, 16, 21
Punishment 13, 18, 21, 24-25

Recreation 21, 23
Religion 22-23
Revolts 28-29

Slave auctions 4, 10
Slave ships 8
Slavery 5, 9, 13, 16, 27
Sugar 5, 6, 7, 16

Tobacco 5, 7, 16
Triangular Trade 7
Tubman, Harriet 26
Turner, Nat 29

Underground Railroad 26

Washington, Booker 14
West Indies 6
Whitney, Eli 16
Women 8, 24
Working life 16-17, 18-19

Picture acknowledgements

The pictures in this book were supplied by the following: BBC Hulton Picture Library 15 (top); Chicago Historical Society 10; Mary Evans Picture Library 22, 25 (top); The Mansell Collection 16-17 (main picture), 26 (lower), 29; The Robin May Collection 17 (inset picture); The National Maritime Museum 9 (top). All other pictures are from the Wayland Picture Library.